Michiel van der Mast

THE HAGUE

87 COLOR ILLUSTRATIONS

ƎB

Bonechi Publishers

◀ The Hague seen from the tower of
St. Jacobskerk.

© Copyright 1980 by CASA EDITRICE BONECHI s.r.l.
Via dei Cairoli, 18b – 50131 Firenze
Telex 58323 CEB

ISBN 88-7009-096-5

Photographs by R. Glaudemans and by VVV, Den Haag,
pages, 4, 10.

Finito di stampare nel mese di Gennaio 1980

Distributed by:
PAAGMAN
Frederik Hendriklaan 217b
DEN HAAG
Tel. 070-543700

HISTORY OF THE HAGUE

The city of the Hague does not owe its origin to a dam built on a river, as is the case with Amsterdam on the river Amstel, nor to a ford (in Dutch: tricht), like Maastricht on the Meuse. It arose in the first half of the 13th century due to the construction of a residence for the Counts of Holland. At that time the Counts of Holland had no fixed place of residence; they travelled from one place to another to administer justice among the people, put down revolts or gather funds for the wars. At Leyden and at 's-Gravenzande, for example, they had houses available to them where they lived for the time necessary for their work. To this end, around 1230, Floris IV began the construction of the various buildings that make up the Binnenhof. His successors, Willem II and Floris V, continued his work. In time the Binnenhof became the permanent residence of the Counts of Holland and successively the seat of the government. Near the Binnenhof, on the site where the St. Jacobskerk was later to be built, stood a small house, probably dating from the 11th century. The arrival of the Count and his retinue of court dignitaries and other officers who, in ever greater numbers, established their homes around the Binnenhof, was greeted by the local population as an excellent opportunity to increase their own activity; they had building materials brought to the site and sold food and drink. As a result of this flourishing economy "Die Hague" grew and became a centre of importance. Even today there is no definite documentary proof concerning the origin of the name. Perhaps the hedge around the hunting reserve of the Count, the Hague wood, is the origin of its name: Die Haghe (the hedge), later Den Haag or 's-Gravenhage. There is even uncertainty about the exact date of the city's foundation. In 1948 the 7th century of the city's foundation was celebrated because in 1248 Count Willem II founded the Binnenhof. Now, after recent studies, it seems that the first works of construction were begun around 1230; this therefore would be the date of its foundation. With other cities the date of birth is taken from the document that bestows, on behalf of the Count, the title of "city". Although the governors of the Hague tried to obtain this privilege until at least the 16th century, it was never granted and the Hague entered history as "the village of villages", or "the most beautiful village in Europe"; yet the Hague of the Middle Ages had a decidedly city-like appearance. It had its own administration, its own law court, a market; while as regards the number of inhabitants, economic activity and the presence of different social classes, it could be considered a city large enough to be compared with other cities. Around 1300 about 1,200 people lived in the Hague, this number had risen to 6000 by the next century.

The houses were not built one alongside the other, lining the streets, for each stood in its own ground. The streets were not paved. During the 15th century the cloth industry flourished in the Hague and of a population of eight thousand, one thousand worked in this sector. These were united in fraternities and corporations, as the other artisans.

The 16th century was a period of great movement. After the complete collapse of the cloth industry, the Eighty Years' War followed in 1568 in which Protestant Holland fought Catholic Spain. The Hague suffered considerably as it lacked any kind of defensive protection and the Spanish were therefore able to enter it without difficulty. Only in 1613, on the initiative of Prince Maurits, was the digging of a surrounding moat begun although, from the military defensive point of view, it had little significance.

In the meantime government meetings were again held in the Binnenhof, as they were before the retreat at the coming of the Spaniards. The population returned to their houses and during the first half of the 17th century the Hague experienced a great flowering. The city was enriched by fine buildings designed by famous architects; the population grew rapidly and around the Spui (the river port) an area full of life and commercial activity grew up. In the course of the following century the economic conditions slowly worsened and not even the arrival of the French brought the prosperity that had been hoped for. In eighteen years six hundred of the eight thousand buildings in the Hague were demolished without others being constructed in their place.

In 1813 the French had just departed and the kingdom of the Low Countries had been created, gradually the reconstruction began. By 1850 the population had grown to seventy thousand and the reconstruction inside the surrounding moat that, until that time, had been the limits of the city was completed. A period of great expansion for the city then began. The changes brought by modern times changed the face of the historic centre, but despite this there remain many characteristic corners and monuments through which the Hague has retained its unique character.

HOFVIJVER AND SURROUNDINGS

Many of the buildings described in this guide are situated in the immediate vicinity of the Hofvijver (the Court Pond). On the right are the buildings of the Binnenhof with the Ridderzaal (the Knights' Hall) in the centre. The Hofweg, in the lower part of the photo, is the result of a city clearance scheme, carried out during the first decade of this century, in which many houses were demolished to ease the traffic situation which was ever more intense in the centre of the Hague. On the lower left is the Buitenhof. Following the street along the Hofvijver we come across, among other things, the Gevangenpoort; we then arrive on the Lange Vijverberg (the little hill of the lake). Walking along paths paved with shells among the trees we do not have the feeling of being in a large and busy city. To the right of the Hofvijver there are two buildings very similar to each other: the St. Sebastiaansdoelen and the Mauritshuis. The dozens of trees that together form the letter L line the Lange Voor-

hout, which is praised by poets and writers as being one of the most beautiful and picturesque corners in Europe. In the upper right hand corner of the photo the contrast between the modern buildings and the surrounding historical environment can be seen. At the end of the Second World War a terrible event happened here: the Allied bombers, on the 3rd March 1945, mistaking their target, struck the Bezuidenhout and this part of the city centre. After the war reconstruction began.

BUITENHOF

The Buitenhof (the Outer Court) once had a completely different appearance from that which it presents today. What was once an area surrounded by walls, accessible only by means of the Gevangenpoort and some narrow passageways, is now a rather spacious square. The Buitenhof was originally the place where the blacksmith, the lockmaker, the carpenter and falconer lived and was also the stables of the

Count and later the Princes of Orange when they lived here. Particularly during the festivities of the "May tournament" or on the occasion of the procession of the Archer's Corporation, when there was a huge crowd of spectators, the Buitenhof must have had a very lively appearance. The part of the Binnenhof that faces the Buitenhof, the left side, was the so-called "Stadtholder's Quarters" which was built in the first half of the 17th century to house the family of the Princes of Orange.

THE STATUE OF KING WILLEM II

It may seem strange but this statue is an identical copy of an already existing monument in the city of Luxembourg. In 1884 the people of Luxembourg had erected an equestrian statue to the memory of King Willem II in recognition of everything that the king had done for their country. In 1924 a copy of this statue, the work of A. Mercier and V. Peter, was placed in front of the Binnenhof, substituting another statue of the same king that had been sold to the city of Tilburg, where Willem II had lived for some time.

HOFVIJVER

The Hofvijver and its immediate surroundings offer an enchanting view at any time of the year. In the background is the Korte Vijverberg, while to the right the buildings of the Binnenhof are reflected in the water. The appearance of this group has changed considerably in the course of the centuries. Of the medieval buildings the Ministerstorentje (the Minister's turret) has survived, perhaps from 1479, it is seen to the right behind the little island. The hall of the assemblies of the States General of Holland was built between 1652 and 1657 from designs by Pieter Post, to the left of the square tower (the Mauritstoren). It is now used for meetings of the Upper Chamber (the Senate). The other buildings that face onto the Hofvijver were all built between the 19th and the beginning of the 20th centuries in the place of previous buildings. Various theories exist about the origin of the Hofvijver. According to some this was an already existing pond among the sand dunes which was made deeper in the 14th century, enlarged and squared at the sides. The sand from the excavations was thrown out of the lake thus creating the Vijverberg (the hill of the lake). It is possible that the Lange Vijverberg owes its name to this. Others maintain that the double moat that encircled the Binnenhof was further excavated to create the lake on that side. Finally the lake was enlarged in size.

The Hofvijver provided many opportunities for recreation; apart from boat rides during the summer and ice-skating during the winter, during the 16th and 17th centuries water tournaments were held here. To the great enjoyment of the public two boats, each with a team of rowers, were set one against the other; on the poop of each there was a man armed with a shield and a long pole with which he tried to knock his opponent into the water. During the 17th centuries to celebrate important festivals the so-called "Fire Theatres" were built on the Hofvijver. In the evening these were lit with thousands of tapers, releasing the spectacular effects of vast quantities of fire-works. The reflection of the light in the water gave the scene an even more festive appearance.

On several occassions the Hofvijver has been the object of study in an attempt to resolve the problem of space, difficult here as in every other city. Even though to fill in the lake would cause an irreparable loss to the city's appearance... an underground garage was planned there at one time, and at another, the enlargements of the government offices were supposed to have been built there. None of these projects were carried out.

BINNENHOF RIDDERZAAL

The Ridderzaal (Knight's Hall) was originally built as a hall for feasts and receptions, attached to the residence of the Counts which stands behind it and was built slightly earlier (around 1230). Historians are not in complete agreement as to who truly built the Ridderzaal. It is known, more or less, that the "Great Hall" was built for Count Floris V (c. 1280), but now there is also reason to believe that his father, Count Willem II, had a hand in it. (c. 1230). The Ridderzaal, both in a figurative and a literal sense, is the centre of the Binnenhof. The interior with its oak roof, 27 metres high, is numbered among the largest of the secular Gothic creations in Europe. During this century everything possible has been done to preserve the building. This makes it even more difficult to believe that there were centuries when the Ridderzaal was completely abandoned. Pictures from the 17th and 18th centuries clearly show the cracks in the wall and the grass growing between the bricks. The interior looked rather like a covered market with, among other things, the stalls of book-sellers in the middle. From 1709 onwards the lottery was drawn here. Under the French (1795-1813) the lottery was abolished and military drill took place here during the winter. During the 19th century the Ridderzaal was used as a deposit for the State Archives and finally it was decided to demolish the building; fortunately this never happened. From 1898 to 1904 serious restoration work was undertaken, during which the Ridderzaal and the nearby Count's Quarters were brought, as nearly as possible, back to their original state. The wooden ceiling, for example, was completely reconstructed.

REPRESENTATIVES' MEETING HALL

The south wing of the Stadtholder's Quarters was completed between 1777 and 1790. Prince Willem V employed the architect Ludwig Gunckel to include a dance hall in the project. For some time this hall has been used for the meetings of the House of Representatives.

PRINSJESDAG

When the restoration of the Ridderzaal was completed in 1904 by way of inauguration the Opening of the States General—the Opening of Parliament—was held there. Every year this occasion, on the third Tuesday of September, is the cause of great activity and liveliness in the Hague. The golden carriage of the royal couple leaves the Lange Voorhout Palace escorted by the military corps, musical bands and the local authorities in a procession that arrives at the Binnenhof where, in the Ridderzaal, the Queen makes the Crown's speech before the States General.

STADTHOULDER'S QUARTERS

The Stadtholder's Quarters, the work of Peter Post from the middle of the 17th century, is now the meeting place of the First Chamber—the Senate. In the corner is the Mauritstoren (about 1600) and to its left is the extension of the Stadtholder's Quarters, from about 1620. Directly above it, still to the left, are the further extensions of these Quarters, carried out in the 18th century and now used for the meetings of the Second Chamber—the Representatives.

FOUNTAIN

In September of 1885 a monumental fountain was erected in the square in front of the Ridderzaal. It was a gift to the country by Victor de Stuers, one of the great promoters of the restoration of the monuments of Holland, in the name of 86 citizens of the Hague who had paid its cost of about 4,600 florins. It was a token of appreciation for the restoration of the Ridderzaal, begun in 1876. The fountain, in neo-Gothic style, is in wrought iron with a bath of granite; it was designed by the architect and restorer P. J. H. Cuypers. On top of it stands a bronze portrait of Count Willem II who played a large part in the creation of the Binnenhof. After several years of absence for restoration the fountain was replaced, marking the "Year for the Monuments" in 1975.

GRENADIERS-POORT

There are three entrances to the Binnenhof. The one in the photo, the Maurits or Grenadierspoort (Grenadiers' Gate), is located to the east, near the Mauritshuis. This entrance was built in 1633-1634 by Matser Joris Cornelisz Faes, replacing the Oostpoort, which previously stood on this site. In front of it was a drawbridge which was replaced by a fixed bridge when the moat around the Binnenhof was filled in 1862. On the east side is the Middenpoort—or Stadthleder's poort (the Middle or the Stadtholder's gate)—which was built in late Gothic style and could be used by the Stadtholder alone. Finally on the south side is the Hofpoort or Haverzakpoort, whose present appearance dates from the end of the 18th century.

MAURITSHUIS

The Mauritshuis is a world famous museum. When it was opened in January 1822 visitors could view the collection of paintings on Wednesdays and Saturdays.
The only condition was that they should be decently dressed and that children should not be brought with them. Since then much has changed; now the museum is open daily and children are just as welcome as adults. The collection of mainly 17th century art has increased from the hundred or so paintings in 1822 to ten times that number. Among these are famous paintings such as the "Anatomy Lesson" by Rembrandt (top right) and "the Bull" by Paulus Potter (below right). Not only the collection of paintings is worth a visit but also the building which houses it. It was built between 1633 and 1644 by Pieter Post from designs by Jacob van Campen; it had been commissioned by Johan Maurits van Nassau Siegen, a cousin of Prince Maurits and of Prince Frederick Hendrik. It is a fine example of the classical architecture of our country. This style takes its motifs from Neo-Classical antiquity as may be seen in the large orders of pilasters surmounted by a triangular pediment.

ST. SEBASTIAANS-DOELEN

Less than a hundred metres away from the Mauritshuis (pp. 12, 13, 14) is the St. Sebastiaansdoelen (p. 15), built in the same neo-Classical style. It was originally a meeting place for the corporation of St. Sebastiaan, one of the two corporations of archers who, from the 15th century, were responsible for law and order in the Hague. The corporation of St. Joris (St. George) was for the elite for, among other things, they used the very expensive crossbow. The archers of St. Sebastian, on the other hand, used the ordinary bow. After 1580 the Corporation of St. Joris lost its military nature and had become an exlusive society. In 1538 the Corporation of St. Sebastian was authorized to use firearms and continued its role as the civic guard. Due to the ever-increasing number of members it was necessary in the 17th century to construct a large building. The first stone was laid in 1636 and soon, on the corner between the Korte Vijverberg and the Tournooiveld, the new head-quarters rose up, designed by Arend van 's-Gravensande; it was used for festivals and meetings. For shooting practice targets were set up behind it. The name derives from this: St. Sebastiaansdoelen (doelen means targets). When the corporation was disbanded in 1795 the local museum, amongst other things, was located here.

LANGE VIJVERBERG

The character of the Lange Vijverberg was completely altered during the 18th century when the rich land-owners wished to enlarge and embellish their houses, as was the custom of the age. The houses with stepgable façades gave way to large buildings with smooth façades and flat eaves.

JOHAN VAN OLDEN-BARNEVELT

From high on a pedestal the grand pensionary, Johan van Oldenbarnvelt, stares across the water of the Hofvijver towards the Binnenhof. There, in front of the Ridderzaal, he was beheaded in 1619. The political differences between him and the Prince Maurits had led to this tragic outcome. The bronze statue was carried out by L. O. Wenkebach and unveiled on the 14th October 1954. In the background is a superb Louis XIV façade, a creation of the Frenchman Daniel Marot, who was employed in 1715 by Cornelis van Schuylenburch to construct this house. It is now the official residence of the German ambassador.

NEDERLANDS KOSTUUM-MUSEUM

The most important architect in the Hague during the 18th century after Daniel Marot was Pieter de Swart. From 1755 to 1756 he built no.s 14, 15, 16 along the Lange Vijverberg so as to form an architectural whole. No.s 14 and 15 contain the Dutch Museum of Costumes (Nederlands Kostuummuseum) which is made up of an enormous collection of costumes, articles of dress and accessories (umbrellas, trimmings etc.) dating from the second half of the 18th century down to our own day. A rare example of older fashions is a boy's doublet made of velvet. The creations of the modern Dutch and French designers such as Cardin, Dior, Heymans and Holthaus are widely represented. The models, dressed in the costumes of the different periods, are placed partly in reconstructed period settings and partly in show-cases. In the basement are most interesting antique dolls' houses, particularly fascinating for children.

GEVANGEN-POORT

Until 1923 the Buitenhof could only be reached by passing through the Gevangenpoort (Prisoners' Gate), coming from the Plaats. In that year the houses which stood between the Gevangenpoort and the Hofvijver were demolished to make way for the present road that links the Spui and the Kneuterdijk. At the entrance, dating from the 14th century, a 15th century prison was built on; it became famous particularly for the fact that the De Witt brothers were imprisioned here before they were barbarously slaughtered (page 20). In the 1800's the Gevangen-poort was nearly completely demolished as it was considered an ugly building and it brought to mind sad events, but particularly because it got in the way of the plans for new roads. Today the Gevangenpoort attracts many visitors; thousands of people go to see the museum of torture instruments which is located inside.

PLAATS

Plaats is the old word for a large square. In the 11th century, a long time before the Binnenhof was built, some country houses must have stood on the Plaats. The Gevangenpoort is the only surviving medieval building. The large bronze statue, which was uncovered with great ceremony in 1918, represents Johan de Witt in the robes of grand pensionary. He led the Republic of the Low Countries from 1653 until 1672. In that year the struggle between the supporters of the Republic and those of Orange grew more intense and finally arrived at a dramatic conclusion. Cornelis de Witt, the brother of Johan, had been imprisoned in the Gevangenpoort, accused completely falsely of plotting to kill Prince Willem III. When Johan went to visit him he was unable to return to his house on the Kneuterdijk due to the huge crowd that had gathered. The doors of the prison were forced open, the Archers of the Hague who were on guard did not intervene, and Cornelis and Johan de Witt were dragged outside by the maddened crowd and killed.

JOHAN DE WITTHUIS

The house of Johan de Witt near the square was not, as one may think, commissioned by the grand pensionary himself but by Mattheus Heefft who, as deacon and burgomaster of Doesburg, had a seat in the States General and consequently stayed often in the Hague. The house was built between 1652 and 1655, probably from plans by Pieter Post. Johan de Witt rented the building from 1669 until his death in 1672.

PALEIS KNEUTERDIJK

At the beginning of the 18th century Johan Hendrik, Count of Wassernaeroobdam, owned several houses on the Kneuterdijk. He was the grandson of Admiral Jacob van Wassernaeroobdam to whom a memorial stone in the choir of the Jacobskerk is dedicated. Johan Hendrik was also struck by the wide—spread craze for destruction and reconstruction that fundamentally altered the appearance of the Voorhout and of the Vijverberg. He demolished his houses and, in 1717, began the construction of a palace in their place, on the corner of two streets, in the manner of Daniel Marot. Exactly a century later there was a new wave of building activity to enlarge this house which was "important, well constructed and surrounded by hedges." King Willem I had bought the building in 1816 as the residence for his son, the future Willem II, and his son's wife, Anna Paulowna. Among other things a fine ballroom was added. In contrast to the sumptuous furnishings of the palace the king's room gave the impression of great austerity; four and a half metres square it contained a simple iron camp bed.

KLOOSTERKERK

The Kloosterkerk stands on the corner of Parkstraat and the Lange Voorhout; it was originally part of a Dominican monastery founded around 1400. The church is composed of a central nave and terminates in a choir. In 1540 the building was extended to the south with the addition of an aisle and three adjacent side chapels. In the photo of the interior the oldest part may be seen on the left and to the right the new part. During the unsettled times of the Reformation in the second half of the 16th century many of the Catholic religious buildings were demolished. Of the monastery of the Dominicans, which was demolished in 1583, only the church was spared because it could be adapted for other uses. The church was first used as a stable and later as a foundry for cannon where the gun-barrels were prepared. In 1617 the nave was altered to be used as a church for Protestant worship but the choir, which was separated by a wall from the rest of the building, was used until 1665 as a cannon foundry.

LANGE VOORHOUT

To the right of the Kloosterkerk is one of the few remaining houses left in the Hague with a stepped roof, it dates from the 17th century. It was built in 1620 as the house of the cannon founder who had his workshop in the choir of the Kloosterkerk. It got its name, "Pageshuis," when Willem IV lodged his pages there in 1748. In the 16th and 17th centuries there must have been many of these houses with stepped roofs along the Voorhout which gave place in the 18th century to the austere patrician residences, such as that of Adrienne de Huguetan, built by Marot in 1734-1736. Since 1819 the Royal Library, the Koninklijke Bibliotheek (above right) has been located there. In 1760 Pieter de Swart was employed by Anthony Patras to build the house (lower right) that is now famous as it is the arrival and departure point for the royal procession on the Prinsjesdag (page 10).

KONINKLIJKE SCHOUWBURG

The Koninklijke Schouwburg (the royal theatre) is a 19th century hall with an evocative atmosphere on the Norte Voorhout where the "Haagse Comedie" performs. The building itself goes back to the 18th century, it was the only part actually carried out of a palace of grandiose proportions planned by Pieter de Swart. Shortly after completing this wing of the palace in 1765, its commissioner, the Duke of Nassau-Weilburg, died and therefore the remaining works were cancelled. The building's use as a theatre dates from 1804.

MUSEUM MEERMANNO WESTREENIANUM

This museum is situated on the Prinsessegracht in a house that was originally in early 18th century style but was later reconstructed with a neo-Classical façade during the restorations of the second half of the 19th century which were made in accordance with the will of the owner, W. H. J. Baron van Westreenen, who died in 1848 leaving his house, his collection and his entire estate to the State, on the condition that it was

made into a museum. The organization of this museum has been somewhat altered since it was opened in 1852 but it is still possible to see the Egyptian statues, the Greek and Roman vases, the family portraits and a fabulous library with a collection of ancient manuscripts that is justly famous. Since 1960 this has been set out in the Book Museum (Museum van het Boek) together with an imposing collection of ancient and modern prints.

VIJVERHOF

The detail of this building, situated at the far end of the Buitenhof, which is particularly striking is the red of the façade given to it on the completion of the restoration in 1975. This choice was dictated by following two 18th century paintings in which the building is minutely reproduced. If we recall the appearance of the Mauritshuis (page 12), the St. Sebastiaansdoelen (page 15) and the Johan de Witthuis (page 20 it is abvious that this building dates from the same period. The first owner—it seems likely that he did not even live there—was an army captain named Wederholt. He had bought the house on this site in 1642 and was permitted to demolish it on the condition that he build another in its place within 18 months. In 1766 Willem V bought the building to house his art collection which up to then was located in the Stadtholder's Quarters of the Binnenhof.

GROENMARKT

From Gravenstraat, which leads to the Buitennhof, we can take a good look at the Groenmarkt where, until the middle of the last century, a daily vegetable market was held. Here there are examples of every possible architectural style. To the left, at the far end, is the Gothic St. Jacobskerk in front of the old City Hall in Renaissance style, with 18th century additions. 19th century and Art Nouveau architecture from the end of the 19th century are also found here, even though they are not seen in the photograph. The building with a tower at the far end, on the right, is by H. P. Berlage, the famous architect. On the extreme right is the restaurant-cafe "'t Goude Hooft" where, during the summer, the sun may be enjoyed on its terrace. It dates from the 17th century but was reconstructed in 1934 in neo-Antique style. In the middle of the Groenmarkt the City Information Centre and Hall of the City Council are examples of modern architecture. They were designed by P. Zanstra and were opened in 1972.

OUDE STADHUIS

In 1975 the reopening of the Old City Hall in the Groenmarkt was celebrated. Six years of restoration were required to return it to its ancient splendour. The Old City Hall is used for marriages and official receptions. Together with the City Council Chambers (page 29) it constitutes once again the centre of local government in the Hague. In 1564 and the following years the Mayor of the Hague had his new residence constructed. Although the dimensions are small the building is a jewel of the Renaissance art of construction (on the right in the photo). Another wing was added in 1733 due to, among other things, an increase in the number of administrative personnel; the lines of this part are flatter than those of the 16th century building which is more elaborate and decorated with much sculpture. The two parts of the building, however, do not jar with each other.

BURGO-MASTER'S ROOM; VIERSCHAAR

In the Old City Hall there are some superb rooms such as the old Burgomaster's Room, in the 18th century part (photo left). The "Vierschaar," in the 16th century wing, was the chamber where justice was administered. At the back of this room the bench of the echevin (medieval judge) can be seen along with a painting, dated 1671, which represents the judgement of Solomon, an obviously appropriate subject. The "Vierschaar," in its original sense, was an area delimited by four benches, where the Courts sat.

ST. JACOBSKERK

For centuries the bell-tower of the St. Jacobskerk was a land-mark for travellers in the Hague. It also served as a look-out tower to give timely warning of the approach of an enemy or of the start of a fire. Every half hour the watch-men from the bell-tower sounded the trumpets, in this way it was certain that they never fell asleep. The last watch was relieved on the 1st of January 1884.

This bell-tower is characterized by its hexagonal structure; it was buiit between 1420 and 1423 and is unique in Holland. The original Gothic steeple disappeared years ago. In 1539 a fire caused serious damage to the church as well as to the nearby houses. It was decided to rebuild the spire in contemporary style. In 1957 the building was newly completed, in the 16th century Renaissance style, though rather more squat.

This large church (also known as the "Grote Kerk") is made up of different styles that date from the late 14th century (the latter part of the east transept), the middle of the 15th century (the remaining part of the nave), with certain 16th century additions (choir). The transept to the east of the choir is made up of three side aisles at right angles to, and as high as, the central nave. This type of interior construction, called the "Haagse Halle-type," is also found in the nearby Kloosterkerk (side aisles as high, and often as wide as the central nave).

THE STAINED GLASS

The stained glass of the St. Jacobskerk was lost in the great fire of 1539. The church was restored but the glass was made from new designs. When, six months after the fire, Charles V honoured the Hague with a visit, he decided to donate a window to the church. Only in 1547 was this promise fulfilled; the Emperor's example was followed by many others. At length, due to the damage of continuous deterioration, only two large fragments remained of these windows which were at first put together in a single window. In 1914 the two windows were again reconstructed using the original glass: one is the window of Charles V of 1547 (above right), the other is the window of the Hofkapel (the Court chapel) Canons, of 1541. Both are situated in the choir. Reproduced above left is the window of Jan de Bakker, designed by Max Nauta and ceremoniously uncovered in 1930. Jan de Bakker was one of the first to be burned in Holland for his religious convictions (1525).

VAN WASSENAER-OBDAM

In 1667 in the choir of the St. Jacobskerk a monument was erected in memory of Jacob van Wassenaer-Obdam, the supreme commander of the fleet of the Low Countries which was defeated by the English at the Battle of Lowestoft, where he also lost his life. The funerary monument in marble was erected at a cost of 12,000 florins, an incredible figure for those times, and the work was carried out by the sculptor Bartholomeus Eggers. As van Wassenaer was buried at sea this is not a true funeral monument. Surrounded by statues that symbolize his glory, Jacob van Wassenaer stands beneath a baldachino which rests on four columns. At his feet there are the figures of four women who represent respectively Prudence, Daring, Faith and Sagacity.

THE BENCH OF THE GOVERNMENT AUTHORITIES

This wooden bench, carved with angels, drapes, coats of arms and flower motifs, dates from 1647 and is known as the "Bench of the Government Authorities" because in the past the government authorities sat there.

THE TOMB OF VAN HESSEN-PHILIPSTHAL

Philips, Count of Hessen-Philipsthal, was born in 1665. He spent a good part of his life in military campaigns abroad. During these years he came to be known as a pleasant and courageous man. At the end of his military career he settled in the Hague and built himself a house at the top end of the Scheveningseweg, the Hessenhof, and later called the Buitenrust. In 1721 he left for Aix-la-Chapelle for health reasons where he died unexpectedly. His will stated that he wanted to be buried in his beloved the Hague. For this reason his family bought a tomb in the St. Jacobskerk together with the right to erect a statue in his memory. When the tomb was completed (it seems the design may be by Daniel Marot) in 1723, his remains were placed there. Philips van Hessen is shown in a supine position, he wears armour and in his hand he carries the commander's baton; his wife leans over him in an attitude of concern.

HIC SITUS EST PHILIPPUS LANDGRAVIUS HASSIÆ, PHILIPPSTHAL.
DUM VIVERET, STRENUUS IN BELLO MILES, DUX FORTIS, IN OMNI VITÆ GENERE FACILIS,
COMIS, BLANDUS, ABSQUE OSTENTATIONE INTEGER, SINE FUCO PIUS, VIR OPTIMUS AD
AQUAS SALUBRES, UT VALETUDINEM FOVERET, AQUISGRANUM PROFECTUS, INOPINATA
MORTE ABREPTUS FUIT XVIII. DIE JUNII ANNO 1721 ÆTATIS LXVIII. HUC ADVECTUS
TRAJECTUM AD MOSAM, &, IN TEMPLO D. JOHANNIS DEPOSITUS. POSTEA HAGAM
COMITIS, OLIM DELICIAS SUAS, &, UBI TRANQUILLE EXTREMAM VIGINTI ANNORUM
ÆTATEM TRANSEGERAT, TRANSLATUS, TANDEM HIC CONDITUS, FUIT.
CATHARINA AMELIA A SOLMS LAUBACH SERENISSIMA UXOR PERPETUO
TAM CHARI CAPITIS PERMOTA DESIDERIO, POST CONJUNCTISSIMUM XLII.
ANNORUM CONJUGIUM, HOC   MAUSOLÆUM ÆTERNI
MÆRORIS MONUMENTUM,   PONIT CONJUX CONJUGI.

PALEIS NOORDEINDE

In 1640 the Stadtholder Frederik Hendrik commissioned Jacob van Campen and Pieter Post to carry out much extension work on the so-called "Huis van Goudt." The result was a neo-Classical town palace which, according to descriptions, had a marvellous interior, splendidly furnished with carpets woven with gold, expensive furniture and rare furnishings. By the 18th century the building was in a completely abandoned state. Voltaire, who stayed there for a while, wrote that traces of its earlier splendour could still be made out, but that the rain came in and that the wooden parts of the floors were rotten. Only in 1815 was it restored and once again used as a palace, the residence of King Willem I. Another floor and two side wings at the back of the palace were added. This new floor was badly damaged by a fire in 1948; during the following restorations it was decided to remove this floor and to replace the 17th century façade.

WILLIAM OF ORANGE

On the decision of King Willem II a bronze statue of the "Father of the Fatherland," Prince William of Orange (1533-1584), was erected in 1845. It should be noticed that the Frenchman E. van Nieuwerkerke depicted the prince in the clothes of an heroic commander while in fact William of Orange achieved fame only as a statesman. The artist was inspired by the equestrian statues of the Italian Renaissance.

THE GARDEN

The Hague is rich in gardens, parks, woods and reserves which are open to the public. The garden behind the Paleis Noordeinde, due to its location, is the most central in the Hague. Its present appearance dates from 19th century romantic ideas of the countryside; it was certainly arranged differently two centuries earlier. In the centre there was a circular pond, on opposite sides there were two square areas, each divided by paths of a symmetrical design which were lined with trimmed hedges.

THE MESDAG PANORAMA

The Mesdag Panorama is unique in Holland. In the last century however this kind of entertainment was widespread. In 1880 a "Panorama" was opened in Amsterdam and a year later at least three in the Hague: one in the Bezuidenhoutseweg, one in the Victoria Hotel, at Scheveningen, and one in the Zeestraat, the Mesdag Panorama. The visitor stands in the centre of a circular area. On the walls a stupendous panorama is revealed with the village of Scheveningen, the sea, the dunes, the beach where the fishermen's boats are tied up and the military who perform equestrian drill, the whole is seen from the Seinpostduin. On the first of May 1880 Hendrik Willem Mesdag was given the task by the "Societé Anonyme du Panorama Maritime de la Haye," based in Brussels, to carry out this enormous painting that had a total circumference of 120 metres and a height of 14.

It was impossible, naturally, for Mesdag to undertake the entire work. He was assisted by his wife Sientje Mesdag-van Houten, Th. de Bock and G. H. Breitner who painted respectively the village, the dunes and the sky and the military. They needed only four months to complete the entire scene from the village to the sea; on the 1st August 1881 the Mesdag Panorama was officially opened.

PLEIN 1813, NATIONAAL MONUMENT

In the 19th century many monuments and memorial stones were erected in memory of people and events of national history. To commemorate Holland's liberation from French domination in 1813 countless proposals were put forward as the year 1863 approached; one such was the construction of a National Monument in the Hague. What should have symbolized National Unity became the opposite: endless discussions on the make-up of the Commission responsible resulted in the competition being held only two months before the anniversary. On the 17th November 1863 it was only possible to lay a foundation stone of something that had not yet been planned. The choice for the winning design was similarly drawn out due to learned disputes; finally however the honour fell to J. Ph. Koelman and W. C. van der Waayen Pieterszen. Their monument was constructed in a slightly different way than they had conceived. It was unveiled in 1869, six years after the anniversary. The monument is crowned by the Virgin with a lion, the symbol of the Low Countries, at the base Willem I swears his oath as king; there is also the triumvirate Van Hogendorp, Van Limburg Stirum and Van der Duyn van Maasdam, who led the country until the return of Willem I, and allegories of History and Religion.

MESDAG MUSEUM

At the beginning it was not at all obvious that Hendrik Willem Mesdag (1831-1911) would become a famous painter. By day he worked in his father's bank and in the evenings he took drawing lessons. Although no-one recognized talent in him he decided to leave his job and to dedicate himself entirely to art. His perseverance was rewarded when, in 1870 in Paris, he won a gold medal for a sea view. From that moment on his fame as a painter of sea-scapes was assured; his works are found, among other places, in the Mesdag Panorama and the Mesdag Museum. He used his own wealth not only to help financially other painters but also to create an important collection of paintings, so large that he was obliged to construct a museum, the present-day Mesdag Museum, in the garden of his house. He later gave a good part of his collection to the State. In the collection, the works of the Barbizon School (French landscape painters) are well represented: Mesdag was the first to introduce their works into Holland. He also bought many works by painters of the Hague School; peasants and fishermen by Jozef Israëls, the interiors of churches by J. Bosboom and landscapes by J. H. Weissenbruch, Roelofs, Mauve, Gabriël, Jaap and Willem Maris.

VREDESPALEIS

The High Courts of Justice in the Hague. Shortly after the first Peace Conference held in Huis ten Bosch, in 1899, Andrew Carnegie, the Scottish-American multi-millionaire, made available an enormous sum of money for the construction of a worthy headquarters for the Permanent Courts of Justice which had been created during this conference and were to be situated in the Hague. The idea was that the Court should resolve international disputes peacefully, by discussion, thereby avoiding war. An international competition was held for the design of the Vredespaleis. The first prize was won by the Belgian L. M. Cordonnier, but he and his fellow competitors had to put up with heavy criticism: the designs combined styles hardly new in architecture, and the reasons for the Jury's choice were judged rather banal. In effect, according to the report of the Jury, a major merit was the fact that Cordonnier was inspired by 16th century Dutch architecture. Moreover his project proved too expensive to carry out, so, together with J. A. G. van der Steur, a simplified version of the design was realized between 1907 and 1913. Shortly afterwards the First World War broke out!

SPUISTRAAT
AND PASSAGE

The area around the St. Jacobskerk has always been a centre of commercial activity. Markets where butter, fish, pork or vegetables were sold were everywhere; artisans also lived there who made on order furniture, shoes, earthenware and silver objects. This area of the city has now become a large and modern shopping centre, which includes the Spuistraat. The Passage is an area of covered shops, built in 1885 by the architects J. C. van Wijk and H. Wesstra jr.; the part that opens onto the Hofweg was added during the Twenties.

NIEUWE KERK

In the reconstructed area of the city, around the Spui, is the Nieuwe-Kerk, a bit lost in the middle of all the modern buildings. The church was built between 1649 and 1655 from designs by Pieter Noorwits. Of particular interest is the wonderful construction of the wooden vault. According to legend Pieter Noorwits threw himself from the dome of the church because he had made an error in the construction. Apart from the fact that an enquiry established that he died of natural causes, after three centuries the original roof is still intact.

SPINOZAHUIS AND SPINOZABEELD

On the Paviljoensgracht is a statue of the greatest philosopher born in Holland, Benedict de Spinoza (1632-1677). It is the work of H. Hexamer and is made of bronze; it was unveiled in 1880. At that time it was situated a few metres away from the site where, since 1957, it has stood; nearby is the small house where Spinoza passed the last seven years of his life in a garret and where he gave the last touches to one of his most important works, the Ethics. The house of Spinoza was built in 1646; its first owner was the painter Jan van Goyen, who never lived there. Since its complete restoration in 1977 this house has been a study centre, open to anyone interested in Spinoza's philosophy.

HEILIGE GEESTHOFJE

Facing the Spinozahuisje, behind a long blind wall with the main entrance in its centre, is the Heilige Geesthofje (the little courtyard of the Holy Spirit), a peaceful place in the midst of all the traffic. The courtyard was built in 1616 to relieve needy old people who were able to stay free of charge in the 35 small houses grouped around the courtyard.

HOUTWEG

During the 19th and early 20th centuries many of the canals in the Hague were filled in due to, among other reasons, the smell; however, in the picturesque zone to the east of the Lange Voorhout the houses on the Smidswater, the Nieuwe Uitleg (to the right) and the Houtweg (in the middle) are still reflected in the water of the canals.

NIEUWE UITLEG
AND
SMIDSWATER

In the first quarter of the 18th century the city spread out along the Prinsessegracht, the Kanonstraat and the Nieuwe Uitleg. A great number of the fine houses that were built at that time are still there today. There are thirteen large dwellings on the Prinsessegracht, including the Meermanno Westreenianum Museum (see pages 26 and

27). Behind these aristocratic houses are the gardens and the mews for the carriages, these give on to the Jan Evertstraat. The Portuguese Synagogue, constructed in 1825 from designs by Daniel Marot, is also here. The two imitation 18th century houses (above left) are in the Nieuwe Uitleg. Nearby, at number 16, lived Mata Hari. In 1903 she settled in Paris where she was a triumphant success as a naked dancer; as a highly paid courtesan she had relationships in the highest social circles. In 1917 she was accused of spying for the Germans, condemned to death, and shot. When her house on the Nieuwe

Uitleg was opened to the public for a few days in 1918, it was like a tide. Ladies and gentlemen in search of the curious were divided into small groups and allowed to enter, as reports one of the newspapers at the time.
On the other side of the Nieuwe Uitleg we see the Smidswater. The house at no. 26 shows both neo-Gothic and Jugendstil elements. The Jugendstil, which had its great flowering right after the turn of the 20th century, is recognized by the use of very curious entwining ornamental elements such as that of the balustrade of the two superimposed bay windows.

DEN HAAG CENTRAAL

For more than a century the Hague has had two railway stations. In 1843 the "Hollandse Spoor" station was built, fifty years later it was replaced by the present building. In 1870 the "Staatsspoor" station was opened with a great festival held on the platforms. The first station was intended for internal communications, for links with Amsterdam and Rotterdam. The second was linked to the European network, via Utrecht. In March 1945 when, due to a fatal mistake, the allies bombed the Bezuidenhout, the Staatsspoor was undamaged. The area was so badly destroyed that after the war very extensive plans were made for its reconstruction, which included the building of a new station that would replace the old Staatsspoor. A hundred years had passed since the construction of the station, when it began to be demolished to make way for the enormous Den Haag Centraal, designed by the architect K. van der Gaast. This is the centre for three types of public transportation: the train, which is reached through the main entrance on the ground floor; the tram and the bus which depart from an area raised above the platforms. The official opening of the station took place in September of 1973 but its construction was only completed in 1976.

The building to the left of the station is the Babylonkomplex, opened in September 1978. Here, amongst other things, there are a hotel, a commercial centre, theatres, offices and underground car parks. Inside the harmonious proportions of the modern, flat, glass-covered exterior and the interior furnishing constitutes an intentional contrast: here one breathes the nostalgic air of the "fin de siècle."

HAAGS-GEMEENTE-MUSEUM

The City Museum of the Hague. In 1855 the "Society for the study pf the history of the Hague" was founded with the intention of creating an historical museum. Eleven years later the "Society for the foundation of a museum of Modern Art" was established and in 1871 the two societies were united and the Haags Gemeentemuseum was created. From 1884 the St. Sebastiaansdoelen (p. 15) has been 'a museum. After the First World War the lack of space became such a problem that the famous architect H. P. Berlage was employed to design a new museum. When he completed the designs in 1921 the result was an enormous cultural centre of which the museum was only a part. The difficult economic situation of the period made it impossible to carry out this ambitious project. Later Berlage himself executed a simplified version of his own project that was opened in 1935. In this building the museum's collection is displayed while in a new wing shows are held. In the Berlagegebouw the visitor should see the Crafts section with the most beautiful pieces in glass, silver and porcelain coming from all over Europe, China and Indonesia; the Music section with European and foreign musical instruments; the Modern Art section, with a superb Mondrian collection. The section "Haagse Historie" offers a picture of the founding and the historical development of the city of the Hague.

CONGRES-GEBOUW

Conference Centre. Berlage's plans for a cultural centre in this part of the city have, to a certain extent, been achieved: near the Haagse Gemeentemuseum the Congresgebouw has stood since 1969; it is the work of the architect J. J. P. Oud. Conferences are held here and so are classical music and pop concerts, theatrical performances and other cultural events.

MADURODAM

The tourists who want to visit Holland in a couple of hours can go to the miniature city of Madurodam. Many of the buildings illustrated in this book, such as the Ridderzaal, the Heilige Geesthofje or the Vredespaleis are reproduced there on a scale of 1:25, together with the other tourist attractions of the cities and places in Holland: the Paleis op de Dam in Amsterdam and the City Hall of Gouda; there are also the famous Dutch factories, the department stores, the motorways the docks and ports, the Schiphol airport and a reconstruction of the Polder countryside. This is a condensation of everything that Holland, in all its variety, has to offer. The proposal to build a miniature city was launched in 1950 by Mrs. B. Boon-van der Starp who wished to send the proceeds of this place of entertainment to the Nederlands Studenten Sanatorium. To bring about this idea a large amount of money was made available by Mr. and Mrs. Maduro of Curaçao, who wanted to dedicate this work to the memory of their son George; he had distinguished himself during the war by his commitment but died in a concentration camp in 1945. The project was brought to completion with the financial support of several industries and institutions. The city council of the Hague made the land available, which extends over in area of 18,000 sq. metres, and the architect S. J. Bouma undertook the design of this extraordinary town. On the 12th July 1952 the opening took place in a very festive atmosphere.

HAAGSE BOS

Count Floris IV built his residence, the future Binnenhof, on the edge of the Haagse Bos (the Hague wood) which at that time covered a much larger area than it does today. The Korte and the Lange Voorhout meant literally "in front of the wood" and the "beginning of the wood" (hout means wood), just as the Buitenhof (Buiten: outer; hof: court) and Binnenhof (Binnen: inner). The wood which provided an inexhaustible supply of construction materials and fire-wood, as well as being an ideal hunting area, was quickly raised to being the Count's Domain.

On several occasions the Haagse Bos was on the point of disappearing. During the Eighty Years' War (1568-1648) the States General of Holland decided to cut down the wood to subsidize the war fund. When the petitions from the Hague were not sufficient Prince William of Orange was still able to arrive in time to prevent this violence against nature. In 1943, however, a large part of the Haagse Bos was destroyed during the preparations of the German lines of defense, the Atlantic Fortifications. But immediately after the war reforestation was undertaken, thanks to which no traces of past damage are to be seen. There were times when the peace of the Haagse Bos was regularly broken, for example, during the nights of Pentecost when the "festival in the wood" was held, with much noise and much drinking. The clang of swords was also sometimes heard: Casanova, who stayed for some time in the Hague, relates in his memoires how he fought a duel with a Frenchman in the Haagse Bos, and how, naturally, he emerged the victor.

HUIS TEN BOSCH

In 1645 Pieter Post was commissioned to design a new summer residence for Amalia van Solms in the Haagse Bos. The result was a small, simple palace made up of a central hall with a dome, surrounded by several rooms. When her husband, the Stadtholder Frederick Hendrik, died in 1647 Amalia van Solms decided to dedicate the Huis ten Bosch to his memory. Under the leadership of Jacob van Campen a great number of artists were put to work in the Oranjezaal (the domed hall) to eternalize in huge paintings the honours and glory of her consort. The palace was enlarged at the behest of Prince Willem IV between 1734 and 1739 with two large side wings and a portal, designed by Daniel Marot.

HOFWIJCK

At one time many country houses were built around the Hague for those who, every now and again, wanted to withdraw from the worries of every-day life. Hofwijck, in Voorburg, was completed between 1640 and 1642, from designs by Pieter Post. The man who commissioned and occupied this country house was the poet and statesman Constantijn Huygens. His son Christiaan, who is world famous as the inventor of the pendulum movement in clocks, also lived for some time in the Hofwijck. Many interesting exhibits concerning their lives and work may be seen in the Huygensmuseum, arranged in the Hofwijck.

CLINGENDAEL

In the last quarter of the 17th century Philips Doublet jr. transformed the property that had been bought by his father into a more splendid complex than it had ever been: the gardens were enlarged and planted in Baroque style, the same style as that which Louis XIV had wanted for his gardens around the Palace of Versailles; they were laid out in a symmetrical manner with flower-beds and finely cut hedges with statues and large vases. In the early 19th century, under the direction of J. D. Zocher, the garden was altered into a park in romantic English landscape style with large meadows and well distributed clumps of trees. The house, built in 1680, also underwent considerable changes. Since 1955 the Clingendael Estate has been open to the public. Particularly noteworthy is the Japanese Garden where countless Japanese plants and flowers grow (photo above).

GEDENKTEKEN

Due to the French occupation (1795-1813) the family of the Princes of Orange went to live in exile in England. On the 30th November 1813 Prince Willem VI, later king with the name Willem I, returned to Holland. On a site, as near as possible to the landing-place, on the beach of Scheveningen, an obelisk was erected in 1865, the work of J. M. van der Made and A. Roodenburg. On the pedestal is written: God saved Holland —the People give thanks—30 Nov. 1813-24 Aug. 1865.

SCHEVENINGSE PIER

In place of the Scheveningse Pier, which was opened in 1901 but destroyed by a fire during the Second World War, a new pier was begun in 1959. Since 1961 the tourists have been able to find a wide variety of entertainment there.

KURHAUS

The building that stands out most in the bathing area of Scheveningen is the Kurhaus, designed by the Germans

J. F. Henkenhaff and F. Ebert. Shortly after it was completed in 1886 it was destroyed to its foundations by a fire. Nine months later it had risen again, though in a slightly different version. The two side wings were a hotel. In the central part was the Kurzaal which was used for concerts and other cultural events. In 1976 its complete restoration was begun during which the two side wings were completely demolished and then reconstructed. The Kurhaus, opened in 1979, as well as being a hotel, contains lecture halls and restaurants and the small tent-shaped buildings on the seafront which are a casino.

SCHEVENINGSE VISSERSHAVEN

The fishing port at Scheveningen. During the 19th century there was no port here so the fishermen of Scheveningen literally stranded their boats which were then dragged onto

the beach by horses. After no less than 75 years of planning, second thoughts and more planning, it was finally decided, in 1899, to begin the construction of the port that was completed in 1904. The new port immediately revealed every kind of defect. The movement of the waves was so strong that during a storm the boats would not have been safe at all; above all it was too small to contain the entire fishing fleet of Scheveningen. It was therefore decided to dig a second port (illustrated left) that was opened with great festivities in 1931.

DUINRELL

At the foot of the Wassenaar dunes the Duinrell Estate spreads out; in the 18th century it belonged to Jonker de Jonge van Ellemeet. Contemporary descriptions give a picture of how it must have looked at that time. The house was completely surrounded by a garden which was laid out symmetrically, as at Clingendael. There were statues carved in stone and large vases.

Many different kind of fruit trees and flowers were cultivated on the estate for its residents and their guests. Now it is an attractive recreational park where lovely walks may be taken through the oak and birch woods or across the dunes, which are the highest in the Province of Zuid-Holland. In autumn, on the slopes of the pine woods, the lovers of winter sports ski on a thick carpet of pine needles. In the summer there are boats on the lake for the tourists and the children can go and play in the fun park. There is also a small zoo and an aviary.

INDEX